Gracious WRITER FOR GOD

Grace Livingston Hill

Gracious WRITER FOR GOD

Written by
Betty Steele Everett

CHRISTIAN • LITERATURE • CRUSADE
Fort Washington, Pennsylvania 19034

CHRISTIAN LITERATURE CRUSADE

U.S.A.
P.O. Box 1449, Fort Washington, PA 19034

GREAT BRITAIN
51 The Dean, Alresford, Hants., SO24 9BJ

AUSTRALIA
P.O. Box 91, Pennant Hills, N.S.W. 2120

NEW ZEALAND
10 MacArthur Street, Feilding

Edited by
Robert Delancy

ISBN 0-87508-664-0

Copyright © 1997
Betty Steele Everett

This printing 1997

Photographs of *Grace Livingston Hill* books,
seen on the cover, used by permission.

Grace Livingston Hill books are published by Tyndale
House Publishers under copyright. Tyndale House
Publishers is at P. O. Box 80, Wheaton, IL 60189;
Telephone: 1-800-323-9400.

Contents

Growing Up with Stories

*I*t was April 15, 1865, and bad news was spreading across America by newspaper, telegraph, and word of mouth.

"President Lincoln is dead!"

It seemed impossible that the tall, thin man from Illinois who had just brought the nation through a devastating war was dead. Lincoln had freed thousands of slaves, then decreed no punishment for those who had fought against the Union. He had been relaxing the night before, watching a play at Ford's Theater in Washington, D.C., when he was shot. Now he had died from that wound, and the whole country was in mourning.

Among the many Americans praying for the nation and the Lincoln family at that time was the Rev. Charles Livingston.

Charles was the pastor of the Presbyterian Church in Wellsville, New York. A young man, Charles was praying not only for his country but for someone much closer to him than the Lincolns. His wife, Marcia, was about to have a baby.

"We lost our first child," Charles recalled

sadly. "Percy lived only a short time. Now we are having another child. I pray it will live and be healthy, and that Marcia will be well."

The baby was born the next day, April 16, 1865.

"It's a girl!" the midwife announced. But her joy and elation quickly vanished.

"Get the doctor!" she ordered one of the women who had been helping with the birth. "Tell him this baby's having problems breathing! And tell everyone you meet to start praying for her!"

The baby did live, and knowing personally what the word "Grace" meant, Charles and Marcia named her that.

"Maybe she'll be a writer like her mother and aunt," a few people said. No one even thought of Grace being a preacher like her father and so many others in her family. That was a calling reserved for men!

Grace's mother, Marcia Macdonald Livingston, had written children's stories for Sunday school papers, several books, and even a column for a weekly newspaper for a while.

Yet it was one of Marcia's three sisters, Isabelle, who was the better known writer. Under the pen name "Pansy," she wrote a series of books for children that were very popular.

Isabelle had gotten the nickname "Pansy" years before when she was a child. When she wanted to help her mother get ready for a party she had "helped" by picking all the pansies in the garden for a centerpiece . . . each without a stem!

Grace was only 13 months old when her "Auntie Belle" married the Rev. Alden, who became "Uncle Ross." As Grace grew up, Belle and Marcia were her ideals, and she felt especially close to her aunt.

While Grace was still a child, Belle bought one of those strange new machines called a "typewriter." She would now write her stories on it. It was one of the first Remingtons and had all capital letters. But it was a wonderful time-saving change from handwritten manuscripts . . . and a lot easier to read!

"You may use it, too, Grace," Belle told her. "You can learn to spell words on it."

So the little girl "played" with her aunt's magic machine, learning to spell by typing the words in capital letters.

Grace was a sensitive child with bright blue eyes and soft brown hair. She sometimes had bad moods, but they did not last long. She was also aware of right and wrong, thanks to her parents, especially her father whom she loved deeply.

One Christmas Auntie Belle's gift was an unusual one for a child. It was 1,000 sheets of plain typing paper, along with a challenge.

"See if you can turn these 1,000 sheets of

paper into as many dollars," Belle said.

Grace may not have met that challenge that year with those pages, but she would later turn many thousands of sheets of paper into many dollars . . . and a witness for Christ to thousands of people.

A day for Grace almost always ended with a bedtime story from her mother.

"I can make up stories, too," Grace thought. She began to make up her own tales. Many of these had poor children becoming rich or finding homes with rich people. The houses they moved into were always the same as Grace's dream house.

The Livingstons moved often, and the houses furnished by the churches were often drab, filled with castoff furniture from church members. And these houses were always temporary until Charles was called to another church with another house.

Grace's dream house was large, and was always made of stone. Maybe to her mind stone seemed permanent and strong compared to the houses she temporarily lived in.

Her usual dream house had big windows, a green lawn, spiral staircases, and large fireplaces with cheerful fires burning in them. It was the kind of house Grace dreamed of having herself some day, and until then she gave it to the children in her fanciful stories.

One of the best listeners to Grace's stories

was Auntie Belle. Although the youngster did not know it, Belle sometimes typed the stories as Grace told them.

One of these stories, *The Esselstynes*, became Grace's first book. Like many of her tales, this was about two orphans taken in by a rich couple.

She not only described the house but also the clothes that were bought for the poor children. They were beautiful clothes, perhaps mirroring her own love of fashion, which would last her whole life.

On her twelfth birthday Auntie Belle gave her a special present. Belle had gotten her own publisher to print and bind just one copy of *The Esselstynes*, especially for Grace. It was a regular hard cover book, complete with illustrations.

Auntie Belle gave not only the special book but also some advice to her niece.

"I am your first publisher, Grace, and this is your first book," she told the excited girl. "But from now on you have to write your stories down yourself and find your own publisher. Your mother and I will help you, but you must discipline yourself to your writing."

None of the family realized then how much Grace would need to remember that advice later, or what a prolific writer she would become for the Lord.

Entertainment for children in parsonages

was limited, and Grace was an only child. She learned early to be happy with her stories, books, crayons and pencils. She liked to draw and was good at it.

Although she could amuse herself, Grace never lacked for friends. She was so outgoing and friendly that people liked her . . . and she liked them back.

There was a homemade tennis court in the parsonage yard where Grace and her friends could play. When she got older, she also liked playing chess with her father. She was happy her family was serving God and others, and loved the times of reading together in the evenings after the family's devotions were over.

Charles Livingston's eyes were getting bad, and often Grace would read him the newspaper to save strain on his eyes. She read well, with expression, and from reading aloud to her father she also learned about what was going on outside her own home and community.

Charles was a good pastor. He would go a long way to help someone in trouble or to visit people who needed to talk to a pastor but who lived where there was no church because the people were too poor.

Grace often went with her father on these trips. While they rode, usually in a horse and buggy, she and her father would talk about many things. From these times Grace learned more, including a good understanding of the Bible.

But she went along not just to keep her father company. She entertained the children while her father preached or visited. She told them stories, using different "voices" for the characters. The children loved them and her. These children were the poor ones that Grace always gave "riches" to in her books.

When she was old enough to go to college, she was confused. She wanted more education, but she didn't like the idea of leaving the home and family she loved so much. She finally decided to go to Elmira College.

She did not adjust well to college and being away from home.

"I miss my family so much," she told her friends. "I miss the evenings when we're all together and read to each other! I'm so homesick!"

For a while Grace struggled to live away from her family, but at the end of the first semester she gave up the fight and went home. That love of family, and wanting to be with them, would last all her life.

The young woman still wanted more education, and now began to think seriously of art as a possible career. She still thought of writing as just a hobby, and her family had praised some of her paintings, so she enrolled at the Cincinnati Art School.

But her homesickness was as bad as ever. Even praying didn't seem to help much. She was now 21 years old and had no idea what she wanted to do with her life.

Grace had little time to think about herself and her future now, though. Her father's health was getting worse. He had throat trouble all the time.

"Come down here to Florida where we are," urged Auntie Belle and Uncle Ross. "You know how much the climate here has helped our son. It might do the same for you, Charles."

So in 1886 the Livingstons packed their belongings and took one of the fancy trains that ran to Winter Park, Florida. Charles had been given a church there, and everyone hoped the warmer climate would help him get back his health.

Winter Park was a long way from New York in several ways. Not only was it a long distance away, but life there was a complete change for Grace and her family.

Winter Park was then a new town, planned to be for "men and women of intelligence, culture, character, taste and means."

Both the Livingstons and the Aldens fit right into the pattern, although they may not have had as many "means" as some of the other residents! But it took them a while to get used to the bugs, lizards and spiders that were everywhere outside, it seemed, and often came into the house as well.

"It's so hot and humid, too," Grace thought. "I don't know how father can stand wearing a coat and tie when he preaches every week! I guess it's expected of the minister, though."

There were many good things about Florida, too. The weather was warm enough for one to be outside in the winter, and the brightly colored flowers and oranges growing on the trees were things for Grace to write about to her friends back home.

Actually, except for the "animals" and the climate, life in Winter Park was pretty much the same as it had been up north. Charles did the same work in the church, Marcia kept writing articles and stories, and relatives came to visit. Grace found a nonpaying job she liked— as church secretary, working three days a week with her father.

"If only we could have gone to Chautauqua," Grace said. "It's the first year in a long time that we've missed it."

The Chautauqua organization had been started in 1874. At first it was a sort of camp meeting with outdoor lectures and primitive living along Lake Chautauqua in New York. By the time Grace was in her teens, it had grown and included debates, music and readings as well as lectures, all done by experts in their field. The Livingston and Alden families had made it a part of their summer for years and were well known among the "regulars" who went.

The principle behind Chautauqua was "Education for everybody, everywhere, and in every department of knowledge, inspired by the Christian faith." To meet this high challenge, small groups were organized later around the country to bring "Chautauquas" to small towns.

As that winter got closer, Grace and her mother talked more and more about Chautauqua for the next summer.

"We'll have to get our reservations in soon if we want to get the guest house we like," Marcia pointed out.

"Have you looked at our bank account?" Charles asked gently. "If you consider what it will cost to travel to Chautauqua from Winter Park, and the cost of the Chautauqua itself, I think you will agree we cannot go this summer."

While Grace and her mother could not argue with her father's figures, they did not give up trying to find a way to go. Ideas and suggestions flew back and forth as they did the housework together, but nothing sounded possible.

One day Grace had an idea. "I'll write a book! If I sell it, can we go to Chautauqua this summer?"

Marcia was thrilled with Grace's solution.

She had been urging her daughter to work on improving her writing, and now she would.

Grace went right to work. She did not allow interruptions to upset her and kept coming back to her manuscript after taking time out to read to her father or take part in the family's morning and evening devotions. And she did not miss doing any of her chores in the house!

Grace wrote in longhand in a lined exercise book. *A Chautauqua Idyl* was the imaginative story of some of the flowers, birds, and a brook that decided to have their own Chautauqua.

Grace was a careful writer who wanted to find just the right word and description, and she rewrote the book several times. By December, though, she was sure it was the best she could do.

Marcia read the text and then the two women took turns typing it to send to the publisher. Grace sent it to the same publisher who had printed *The Esselstynes* for her surprise birthday gift years before.

That year Grace and her family were especially glad for all the Christmas activities at the church. Keeping busy with them kept them from wondering and worrying about what was happening to the manuscript at the publisher's. Grace tried extra hard not to think about her story, but it was a struggle.

In January they finally got a letter from the publisher.

"They accepted it!" Grace shouted to her mother, and together they rushed to the church to tell Charles.

"Have you read the contract?" Charles asked quietly.

In her excitement Grace had not glanced at the contract from the publisher, but now she read it aloud and her parents smiled. She had earned enough for them to go to Chautauqua!

That night the family had something bigger than usual to thank the Lord for in their devotions.

Not only did the publisher want to print the book and to pay Grace, but the company had already sent a copy of the manuscript to Bishop John H. Vincent, the founder of the Chautauqua movement. A second copy had been sent to Edward Everett Hale, Chaplain of the U.S. Senate, asking for his views on the book.

Both men wrote back enthusiastically about Grace's work, and the letter from Chaplain Hale became the Introduction for the book.

The publishing company knew the importance of timing and had the book come out just at the opening of the summer Chautauqua meetings. The book, a blue hardback, sold for sixty cents.

When Bishop Vincent spoke the first night of the season, he spoke warmly about the book to the crowd. With Mr. Hale's endorsement, too, the book was a great success. For Grace it was an exciting holiday.

On the way home to Winter Park, Grace thought about another idea she had gotten at Chautauqua for a new book. Auntie Belle had written a series of books about four girls who went to Chautauqua and called themselves "The Chautauqua Girls."

"I'll take quotes from Auntie's books and combine them with verses from the Bible that have the same idea," Grace decided. "I'll have one for every day of the year."

By mid-1888 Grace had finished the book, and Belle wrote a preface for it. *Pansies for Thoughts* was a very small book, easily carried in pocket or purse. It was bound in blue cloth with gold pansies here and there on the cover.

While Grace had enjoyed matching her aunt's words with like ideas from the Bible, she knew she was really a storyteller at heart. She would not write another nonfiction book until 1919, thirty-one years later. In between there would be twenty-eight "story" books!

–2–

Matters of the Heart

*B*ack home in Winter Park, Grace was offered a new job and challenge.

Rollins College had been founded in 1885, and now they were looking for a Physical Education Director.

"Would you consider being that Director?" the president of the college asked Grace. "You would have to meet with the Board for their approval," Dr. Hooker added. "Think about it and let me know next week."

She was working on another book and helping her father at the church, but she decided she could work at the college in the afternoon.

When it came time to meet with the Board, Grace was nervous.

"I'm only a few years older than the seniors at Rollins," she thought. "They will be in my classes, and I'm afraid that might be a problem."

Apparently the Board was not bothered by the small age difference between teacher and students, and they named Grace "Leader in Calisthenics and Heavy Gymnastics."

Since she had always loved sports and being with young people, Grace enjoyed working with the students. Her interest in them went beyond the gym and her classes. She became a sort of unofficial counselor to many of them, urging the men not to take up the dirty habit of smoking (no one even dreamed that a woman would consider smoking!) and to be faithful in going to church.

The biggest problem she faced in her new work came when she decided the girls should have a "uniform" to wear in class. These would be a divided skirt, called a "bloomer," worn with long black stockings and a blouse with a high neck and long sleeves.

She had not expected problems, but when she asked the faculty about adopting this uniform the men were horrified. Was it modest enough? They finally decided to have Grace come back and describe the outfit to them.

She did better than just tell them about the uniform. The outfit included a skirt that could be worn over the bloomers when the girls were outside the gym. Grace went to the big meeting wearing the uniform with the street skirt.

After explaining why the girls needed bloomers for gym class and telling about the outfit she wanted, Grace asked to be excused for a few minutes. She left the room, took off the skirt, and came back wearing the uniform as it would be worn in the gym.

For a few minutes the men were too embarrassed to even look up to see what she had on, but one by one they studied the uniform. At Dr. Hooker's prompting, the faculty finally agreed the outfit was modest enough for the girls to wear even in classes with the boys!

One of the newer, younger professors at Rollins was Dr. Frederick Starr, a science teacher whose speciality was the new study called "anthropology." Frederick was handsome and brilliant, although somewhat eccentric at times, and Grace liked him.

That next summer she and Frederick were at Chautauqua at the same time. They began to play tennis and to go to the lectures together.

Good looking and with a flair about him, Frederick could probably have dated any of the many single girls at Chautauqua, but he preferred being with Grace.

On the other hand, while Grace liked talking to and being with Frederick, she thought of him only as a wonderful friend. As the summer went on, she realized that Frederick was beginning to think of her as more than another friend.

"Perhaps we should spend more time with other people," Grace told him. "Until we get back to Rollins."

There was another male interest for Grace at Chautauqua that summer. Her latest book, *A Little Servant,* had just come out, and everyone at the meetings was coming up to see her and congratulate her. Among them was Rev. Thomas Franklin Hill, called "Frank" by everyone. He was pastor of a church in western Pennsylvania.

"Perhaps you would accompany me to the vesper service tonight," Frank invited, and Grace accepted.

Both Frederick and Frank were intelligent men, but Frank lacked that special flair that seemed to come naturally to Frederick. Yet Frank was a pastor and had other ministers in his family, just as Grace did. He fit in perfectly with both the Livingstons and the Aldens.

When the Chautauqua ended and it was time to say "Good-bye" to Frank, she found it hard to say the words.

"We will write letters to each other this winter," the two agreed before they separated to go their different ways.

The next summer Grace and the two men were all at Chautauqua together again. Now it was a challenge for Grace to keep both men happy, but since they seemed to like and respect each other, sometimes all three went to lectures together.

More and more, though, she found herself leaning toward Frank in the matter of love. By the end of the summer it was obvious he felt the same way toward her, yet nothing was settled between them.

That fall Grace and her family faced another move.

"Your Uncle Ross and I have both been called to churches near Washington, D.C.," Charles told his family.

It never occurred to Grace to stay in Florida when her family was going back north. She wrote a letter of resignation to Rollins College and began to pack.

"You don't have to leave," Frederick told her one afternoon when they were alone in the gym. "You can stay here. Will you marry me?"

As gently as possible, Grace turned down the proposal, appealing to Frederick to keep on being her friend. She predicted great things for him in the future.

"Is it Frank?" Frederick asked. He probably had suspected it was Frank who had won Grace's heart.

Grace nodded. Although Frank had not asked her to marry him, she knew now she could not marry anyone else.

Frederick seemed to take her refusal well, even walking her home. But the next day he left Rollins College and Winter Park.

Grace's prediction of great things for Frederick came true later. He made a world-famous name for himself in the field of anthropology and taught at the University of Chicago for more than 30 years. He traveled around the world to study and was given honors by many countries. But he never married.

As Grace rode north on the train with her family, she finished another book. Words came easily to Grace, and she wrote rapidly. Now this book could come out in time for next summer's Chautauqua.

The town where the Livingstons would live was Hyattsville, Maryland, and the family quickly settled into their natural routine there. An early visitor to the new home was Frank Hill, and by summer his friendship with Grace had grown even stronger. Frank invited her whole family to spend a weekend with him, and asked Charles to preach in his church near Pittsburgh.

Grace dressed carefully that weekend. She knew she was being looked over and evaluated by Frank's congregation, who seemed to know that their young pastor was interested in this vivacious and outgoing young woman. And they were right! By the end of that weekend, Frank had proposed marriage to Grace and she had happily accepted! "I'll give you a ring at Chautauqua," Frank promised.

So that summer of 1892 Grace put the diamond solitaire Frank had chosen on the third finger of her left hand. Then she began to plan a wedding.

December 2, 1892, Grace and Frank's wedding day, dawned clear and cold. The little church in Hyattsville had been turned into a beautiful chapel with flowers, and even a red runner in the aisle where Grace would walk to the altar to be married by her father. She wore a white satin gown and carried a bouquet of lillies of the valley.

After the ceremony, and with the "God bless you" shouts ringing in their ears, the newlyweds took the train to Baltimore to spend their honeymoon. Afterwards they went on to Frank's house and church in Pennsylvania.

The house, furnished by the church for its pastor, was more than adequate for two people. There were three bedrooms, a bath, kitchen, dining room and living room. There was also a large front porch and a carriage house at the back.

It was a house built with a family in mind, but Frank and Grace were not to be there long enough for that. Just a few months after their wedding, Frank was called to a church outside Philadelphia. Grace got ready to move again.

—3—

The Challenges of Life

Frank's new church was Wakefield Presbyterian in Germantown, near Philadelphia. Once more he and Grace began turning a house that wasn't really theirs into a home by using some of their familiar things here and there.

Having grown up in a minister's family, Grace knew what was expected of a good pastor's wife. She attended the worship services, helped with organizations in the church, and went with Frank to call on the sick, both those in their own church and in their neighborhood. She also began Bible studies and planned field trips for the young people. These outings gradually turned into Saturday excursions for the whole family. Both she and Frank were well liked and popular with the people of the church.

Only one thing bothered Grace about her marriage and her husband. She had noticed almost right away that Frank had times of being nervous and jittery. Then he would be all right for a while, but the jumpiness always came back later.

Grace told herself this was just the way Frank was, and tried not to think about it. But one Sunday, almost by accident, she found out the truth.

"You saw me leave before the sermon this morning and take some pills before I went back," Frank reminded her one Sunday afternoon when they were at home alone. "I'm addicted, Grace. Addicted to morphine."

Grace was shocked. She had been worrying that something serious was wrong with Frank, but she had never thought of anything like this.

While Frank had been studying overseas a doctor had given him some pills to ease the pain from the terrible headaches he often got.

"They stopped the pain right away," Frank went on, "but I never asked what they were. And no one told me I could get addicted to them. Grace, I'm sorry I kept this from you. I should have told you right away. I've tried praying and quitting on my own, but nothing helps! I have to have it to keep going!"

No one then knew anything about addiction or how to treat it and rehabilitate the user. As she and Frank held each other tightly, Grace made a decision.

"You should not feel guilty," she told Frank firmly. "You did what you thought was right. And you're a good pastor and husband!"

Frank wanted to keep preaching, and he

and Grace agreed to leave the outcome in God's hands.

"I'll keep preaching until He tells me otherwise," Frank said. "I do think this has helped me understand better the people who have problems they can't handle."

Frank never got over his addiction, but he kept up with his work of serving the church. Grace told no one about their problem until years after Frank died, and then she only told her family.

Despite the pain of knowing Frank's secret addiction, she kept their lives as normal as possible, both at home and in the church. The people who relied on Frank for help and spiritual comfort and guidance never knew of his own personal fight against morphine.

Grace kept on with her writing, along with the church work. She wrote mostly magazine stories and Sunday school lessons. She did not make much money from these but it added a bit to Frank's income, and they were grateful for it.

In September of 1893, Grace and Frank's first child was born. Margaret Livingston Hill was a plump, happy baby, and Grace's mother came to help her take care of the baby during the first weeks.

Despite the extra work of a new baby, Grace kept writing. And her mother was there to give her advice and help with the writing.

Grace's second daughter, and last child, Ruth Glover Hill, was born in January 1898. She was a more relaxed baby than Margaret had been, but she was just as smart.

Now the Saturday outings that Grace had started included the two little girls. Each trip began with prayer, and Frank always planned some time for the people to think about the Lord and their own responsibilities to Him and to each other.

But the summer of 1899 brought the beginning of the end for Grace's marriage. Frank began having severe pains in his side.

"You're having appendicitis attacks," the doctor told him. "I have to be frank with you. There is surgery, but as yet it is quite dangerous. I only recommend it as a last resort. I think you should go on a bland diet and stay off your feet as much as you can."

Frank followed the doctor's advice. He gave up working at the church office as well as visiting. He kept preaching, though. By November, he was much worse.

"I'm going to have to have the surgery," Frank told Grace and the doctor.

The doctor agreed that now it was probably Frank's only chance to survive.

Grace, who had been taking on more and more of Frank's duties and responsibilities at the church, reluctantly agreed. She asked her parents to come to be with her during the surgery, and they came.

When the doctors began the surgery, they found the infection was much worse than they had expected.

"I don't think I'm going to live," Frank told Grace when she brought the girls to see him. He was already so weak he could barely talk. The next day, November 22, 1899, Frank died.

Grace was stunned. She would never see Frank again in this world; never again know his loving touch; never again talk to him in the evening or go calling with him. How could she stand to go on living without him?

Her parents took over, planning Frank's funeral at his church. Grace moved the next few days as though in a fog. She did what she was told to by others, and did it automatically in her sorrow.

After the funeral, however, there were some very practical problems to be faced, now that she was a widow, and she turned to trying to solve them.

"This house belongs to the church," she reminded her mother, who had stayed on to help in any way she could. "They will need it for their new pastor, although they have been gracious and generous and said I could stay as long as I needed to. But I must find somewhere else to live as soon as I can. It's not right to live here now that Frank is no longer their minister."

There was also the problem of making a living now that Frank was gone. There had been a little money from Frank's insurance, but Grace knew that would not last long, and there were no such things as pensions or welfare to help her.

"My writing doesn't earn me enough to live on," Grace thought. "And I'm not trained for any jobs that would pay a woman enough to support a family! And even if I were to find such a job, who would take care of my girls?"

With so many hard questions to find answers to, and feeling all the weight of her responsibilities as a single parent, Grace turned to the Bible for help. She found it in Deuteronomy 33:25, and took the verse for her own. "As thy days, so shall thy strength be." (KJV)

Saying that verse to herself each day helped Grace trust God for the strength to face that one day and its problems. And she turned first to the problem of where she and the girls would live.

"I want to live in a small town so the girls and I can easily walk wherever we want to go," she told her mother. "Some of the church people are looking for me, too. And it has to have good schools, including a college. Then the girls can stay home with me while they're in college, and they won't get homesick like I did."

Grace was thinking years into the future, since her daughters were still babies, but she had never forgotten the pain she had felt of missing her family when she was younger. She had not forgotten the feeling of failure when she came home. She did not want that for her girls.

The Philadelphia area was Grace's choice, and she began looking for a new house and community. She found her ideal town in Swarthmore.

Swarthmore was a quiet town of about 5,000 in the rolling hills just outside Philadelphia. The town was small, the people friendly, and movies and liquor were both banned by local law.

There was also Swarthmore College, with ivy-covered buildings and a grassy campus. It could give Grace the cultural advantages she wanted for herself and the girls. She rented a house in the town.

When the time came to leave Germantown and the house where she and Frank had lived for seven years, and where their girls had been born, Grace broke down. She began to cry and had to be helped and comforted. A happy, important part of her life was unquestionably over; there was no turning back the clock. She had to accept the situation and go on with her life, however the Lord led her.

In a few days she had managed to work

past her worst grief and was ready to face the challenge of her new life without Frank and without income.

As soon as she was settled in the new house, Grace began the daily devotions she and Frank had always had, and which she was used to from her own childhood. It was one way of being both father and mother to Margaret and Ruth. The family also began attending church each week.

Next Grace turned to how to make a living. "Writing is all I know," she thought.

Until now, writing had been a fun hobby, even though she had been paid for her work. Now, though, Grace realized she needed to earn enough money from her writing to pay the rent, buy the groceries, and see that her two daughters were comfortably clothed. It was all very frightening.

Just finding time to write was a major chore for Grace. It became a top priority with her, but she was determined not to let her writing take away from her being a mother to her girls. That, she believed, was her first job.

Grace was homeschooling Margaret, who at five could read and play the piano a little, so she decided she would write while Margaret did her school assignments.

"And Ruth can play with her toys," she thought. She made a playpen in the "office" and was able to keep both girls busy while she wrote nearby.

There was still not enough time to write, so Grace wrote also at night, often until 2 or 3 a.m. This was after she had taken care of the girls, done the housework and cooked the meals. But she always kept her "office" door open for her daughters and, later, their friends who dropped by the house.

To help conserve her precious writing time, Grace hit on the plan of thinking out what she wanted to say the next day just before she fell asleep at night. It is a habit many professional writers use.

At first her writing went slowly, but she kept at it. A break came when a newspaper-man took an interest in what she was doing and got her an assignment to write her weekly Sunday school lesson for the evening paper. Now Grace had her first income she could depend on. It was not a lot, but it made her feel more secure about the writing. It also got her name in front of many readers.

The lessons Grace wrote became popular with the paper's readers and eventually were syndicated in several other papers, adding to her income and popularity.

The 19th century was coming to its end, and people were excited about what the next 100 years would bring to America. Grace was too busy to pay much attention to the celebrations as the 1800s became the 1900s. She was rushing to finish a book.

—4—

Life Begins Anew
in Swarthmore

*T*he book Grace was working on was *A Daily Rate*, which came out in 1900. It began to look as though the new 20th century would be better now for the Hills, despite losing Frank.

Things looked even better when Grace and the girls spent a week with Auntie Belle and Uncle Ross at a cottage by the ocean. It was exactly the relaxing and fun time Grace needed now, and she went back to Swarthmore feeling rested.

Then her father got sick again. This time Charles's illness was very serious. There seemed to be some kind of blockage in his abdomen and the doctors had no idea of a way to help him.

While in Frank's case surgery, although new and dangerous, was at least possible, in Charles's case there was no such surgery known at that time.

"All we can do is keep him comfortable," the doctors told Marcia. By late June, Charles was in bed all the time.

Anxiously, Marcia wrote to Grace. "Come at once or you will likely not see your father alive."

Again Grace prayed that one of the men she loved would be spared by God. She could not see the purpose to all the sadness she was having, but her faith that God did have a reason stayed strong.

When the Hills got to Hyattsville, Charles was obviously very sick.

"Will he be able to talk to me?" Grace wondered to herself. "Will he even recognize me and know me?"

But Charles did know her, and talked a little with her, although it was apparent that it was hard for him The next time Grace went to his room, though, he could not speak to her.

"We'll take turns staying with him night and day," Grace and Marcia agreed.

Hospitals were not the places they are today. Most people were cared for by their families, as best they could, and died at home, usually with family around them.

"Auntie Belle and Uncle Ross are coming to help, too," Marcia said. "And the church people have been so good to us. They've brought so much food. . . ."

"And taken care of my girls," Grace added. It was all those who loved Charles could do now to show their love to his family.

Charles Livingston died on July 5, 1900.

Grace had lost her father less than eight months after her husband had died. It was a hard blow, and she knew how hard it was for her mother, too.

Grace had the answer for her mother, though. Her love of family and keeping it together was the most important thing to her. Marcia would have to leave the parsonage, just as Grace had had to leave her house after Frank died. But the solution for Marcia was obvious.

"You'll come to Swarthmore and live with us, Mother," Grace decided. "That way we will all be together again."

The church members helped with the packing and moving, and in only two weeks Marcia was settled in Grace's rented house in Swarthmore.

For a while it was hard for the two women to share the same house. Both were used to being in charge and doing things their way. Both were also strong-willed and determined women. When they did not agree on how something should be done, they were both ready to argue their side, sometimes loudly. They always agreed, though, that they were merely "discussing" the situation!

Since both Grace and her mother were Christians, and loved each other very much, they knew they had to find an answer to their problem and learn to adjust to the fact they were living in the same house.

"We'll just decide what each of us will do," Grace ruled. "We'll each have our own work to do, and we will do it as we like."

That idea worked, and during the rest of 1900 Grace wrote constantly. It was always Sunday school lessons, articles, or short stories, though. She did not write another novel until 1902, when she had two books published.

Marcia kept reading what Grace wrote and offering her suggestions. She was not an easy critic, finding weaknesses in everything from the way a character talked to the color of the heroine's dress. Her suggestions were always good ones, and apparently Grace did not object to being told what was wrong with her writing and even appreciated her mother's help.

One of the books published in 1902 was *The Story of a Whim*. It attracted a lot of attention from Christian groups and convinced Grace once and for all that novels, not shorter things, were her best kind of writing and the one she should stick to.

The opening of *The Story of a Whim* describes the house Grace had dreamed of since she was a child. The book tells of "the old stone house on the hill."

Over the years, Grace had sketched many pictures of "her" house until she knew exactly what she wanted. She had also drawn up floor plans!

Now, with the income from *The Story of a Whim* and what was left of Frank's insurance money, she was able to think seriously about turning her dream house into a real one.

The first step was to find just the right lot to build on. Grace found it on Cornell Street, right around the corner from where she and her family were living in their rented house. Her new house would be the only one on the block.

"We're ready to build!" Grace told her daughters and her mother. "I have an architect and builder who will do it according to my plans."

In 1904 the house was built—of stone, of course, as she had always wanted.

The house began as a simple three-story one, but over the years Grace had it added to, changed, and remodeled many times until it was a much bigger home, with fourteen rooms. There was plenty of room for everyone in the house.

For her work space, Grace chose a large second-story room. The door was never closed, and the girls were welcome any time. The room was soon cluttered with books and papers, and Grace would write here until her death.

Under the windows of this special room she planted an old-fashioned flower garden. It was planned so that in spring and summer she would be able to smell the flowers as she worked at her desk.

During 1904 Grace's book *Because of Stephen* came out. This was later translated into Swedish, probably the first of many Grace Livingston Hill books to be published in other languages around the world.

The year before the house was built and the new book came out, the church where Grace and her family now worshiped hired a new organist.

"You must meet Mr. Lutz," Grace was told, and she and the new organist were soon introduced.

Flavius Josephus Lutz was fifteen years younger than Grace's age of 38, and was a handsome man, although already starting to lose his hair. He was a charming and talented musician who lived with his parents in a nearby town and came each Sunday to Grace's church to play the organ.

Both of Grace's daughters had been studying the piano—Margaret for several years now. Lutz was interested and asked to hear the girls play.

"Your girls are good students at the piano," he told Grace. "I would like to help them with their training."

She was thrilled at the thought and quickly agreed. "It will be a fine experience for them to study under someone like you."

Not only was Lutz a naturally talented

musician, but he had had good musical training and already had several pupils who came
to his parents' home for lessons.

As the year went on, Flavius and Grace
saw more and more of each other. He came to
the house to teach the girls, and they saw each
other at church each week. As they talked, they
realized they had many interests in common,
including music and books. It was natural that
they should become friends and spend more
time together.

Grace may have been feeling the loneliness
of being a widow who lived only with women.
Not even having her family with her or her
writing would ease it completely. It was nice
to have a man to talk to, especially since Flavius
seemed genuinely interested in helping the
girls with their music.

The two began to see more and more of
each other, and in 1904 Lutz proposed marriage to Grace.

— 5 —

Growing Success as a Novelist

*G*race asked Flavius for time to consider the proposal. She could see many advantages to marriage right now: her girls would have a father figure, someone to give them the male point of view on things; she herself would have a companion who enjoyed many of the same things she did; and Flavius would be able to help the girls even more with their music.

"But I've made my own life now," Grace also thought. "And there is the great difference in our ages, too."

Undecided about what to do, she went to a few close friends to ask their opinions before she gave Flavius her answer.

The friends' advice was almost unanimous: "Don't do it, Grace! It will not be a good marriage." They brought up all the questions Grace herself was worried about, pointing out the problems this marriage could have.

She tried to balance these opinions with the advantages she saw if she married Flavius, and decided to say "Yes." The two were married on October 31, 1904.

It was a bad decision. Perhaps Grace's friends had seen in Flavius what she had not. He had been spoiled by his parents, and even now acted sometimes more like a two-year-old than an adult.

He moved into Grace's home but did not seem to think he should have to work to help with the expenses of running the household.

When Grace suggested that he help with the finances, he replied, "Why? Don't you make enough for both of us?"

Although Flavius was still working as organist at the church, he had no other work or steady income.

Because Flavius was such a good music teacher, Grace decided to help him open a music school in her home. She was able to get him a few students from among her many friends, and the school went on for several years.

Margaret and Ruth kept on with their lessons from Flavius, too. Margaret was one of his best students, and eventually went from the piano to playing the organ.

But life in Grace's dream house no longer measured up to what she had hoped for when the house was built. Flavius showed more and more childish behavior, angrily leaving the room when he did not get his own way. He rarely complimented anyone on anything. He was much better at finding fault with everyone.

Yet he could be charming, too, and the four women learned to stand together when Flavius was critical with any one of them. The other two generations would defend the one Flavius was attacking, and when he was outnumbered, he would stalk off to his room.

Grace kept on with her writing. Although she had been writing for several years and had more than ten novels to her credit, she was still not known beyond the readers of religious publications. The ones who had published her books had been smaller companies, and the books had often been published first as serials in Sunday school magazines.

"I need a publisher with a bigger reputation," Grace told her mother. "Some of my friends say a historical novel would be good. They are so popular now with so many people. That might help me find a bigger publisher."

Marcia agreed. "Why don't you talk to Aunt Margaret?" she suggested, mentioning the woman for whom Grace had named her first daughter. "She may be 100 years old, but her mind is as sharp as ever, and she remembers all the details of something that happened in the family that I think would make a good novel."

Grace had not heard one of the most interesting stories in her own family history. It had happened long before she was born.

A girl in the family had become a last-minute second-choice bride when the expected bride, her older sister, eloped with another man just before the wedding service. The younger sister agreed to take her place. Marcia Schuyler and David Spafford went though with the unusual marriage in order to save face for both their families. Slowly the two discovered they had much in common and fell in love.

"It happened in the 1830s," Grace's mother told her. "Aunt Margaret remembers it well, though. Oh, and you might also like to get in touch with Cousin Henry."

"Cousin Henry" was E. L. Henry, a well-known artist of the day whose speciality was showing how America had lived in the decade of the Schuyler story.

"If he would add drawings for the book, it might help sell it," Marcia added.

All four women went to Johnstown, New York, where Aunt Margaret lived. She made Grace and her family welcome, and eagerly talked for several hours a day until she was too tired to go on. She told Grace all about the circumstances, where it happened, and how things were done back then.

Grace asked a lot of questions, listened closely to the answers, and took plenty of notes about what her aunt was saying.

"I want to dedicate this book to you, Aunt Margaret," Grace told the old lady, but Margaret shook her head.

"No, please dedicate it to your father. He has helped you much more than I have."

Grace did as her aunt asked. *Marcia Schuyler* was dedicated to Charles, "whose companionship and encouragement have been my help through the years."

Naturally, much of the book was from Grace's imagination, but she kept the main plot as it had really happened.

To fill in details about life in the 1830s, Grace spent hours in the Philadelphia Public Library, one of the best in the country, checking old newspapers and magazines. She wanted to know what the people wore, how they traveled, what they ate. She also got in touch with others in the family who might know something about the story.

When Grace felt she had learned all she needed, she spent more time with Cousin Henry, listening to him talk about that era. Sometimes he would make a quick sketch to show her exactly what he was talking about.

Cousin Henry did more than just talk to Grace. He offered to do some drawings to illustrate the book.

"Oh, that would be wonderful!" Grace said. "Could you do one for me to take along when I start the task of seeing publishers with the manuscript? One of your drawings will give the publishers a much better idea of what the book will look like when it is finished."

The whole story was already so complete in Grace's mind that it took her only five weeks to write the first draft of the novel. Once the manuscript met her high standards, she took it, along with Cousin Henry's drawing, and went to Philadelphia.

She made an appointment with the J. B. Lippincott Company, a respected and successful publishing house. To her surprise, she was greeted by Mr. J. B. Lippincott himself.

While Grace sat on the edge of her chair, watching nervously, Mr. Lippincott looked through the manuscript. Then he smiled.

"It has possibilities. We will take the book if you will give us an option on a sequel."

"Oh, yes!" Grace agreed quickly, and signed the contract for a second book with Lippincott.

Grace was thrilled until, a short time later, Mr. Lippincott asked her to come in to see him again. This time he gave her a gentle but very serious talk about what a book—and a writer—needed to be to succeed in the world.

She listened with growing horror. Mr. Lippincott's message was coming through loud and clear, and it was not what she wanted to hear!

According to the publisher, it was all right to have a book with characters of high morals and to have the good people win over the bad ones in the end, but it could not have what he called "Sunday school stuff."

"That sort of thing will not sell books," Mr. Lippincott told Grace firmly. "Take out the gospel!"

Grace was upset, but she had agreed to give Lippincott this book and another, and she would have to honor that contract.

Marcia Schuyler came out in 1908 and the public loved it. *Phoebe Deane* was the sequel, with the same setting and many of the same people in it. Several years later, a third book in the series, *Miranda*, also came out.

Grace had found some success with her historical novels, but she liked writing contemporary books better. With them she could let her imagination go full speed, mixing romance and adventure, and sometimes mystery.

Grace's first Western, *The Girl from Montana*, came out the same year as *Marcia Schuyler*, but from a different publisher. Writing two novels a year was not a new skill for Grace; although some years she wrote only one book, many years she wrote three. She was always thinking ahead to the next book, even while working on the present one.

While her writing life was doing better and better, Grace's life at home was getting worse. More and more Flavius would stomp out of the house when things did not go the way he wanted them to.

At first she worried when he was gone

overnight, but she learned he almost always went to his parents' home, and would come back in his own good time. She stopped worrying about his leaving after that.

Despite their unhappiness, Grace and Flavius did not consider divorce. She knew that a marriage vow, made before God, was to be kept no matter how hard it sometimes seemed to be. Apparently Flavius agreed with her on this.

Now Flavius found another fault with Grace and her writing. "Your name is not 'Hill' any more," he told Grace. "Why are you still using that name on your books? Your name is 'Lutz' now. Why don't you use it now?"

Flavius may not have realized how much he was asking when he asked Grace to use a new name for her writing. Changing her name as author could mean a big loss of sales and readers. Her fans knew her as "Grace Livingston Hill." They might not recognize her as "Grace Livingston Lutz."

There were the libraries, too. Books by "Lutz" would not be put in with those by "Hill," since the books were lined up alphabetically. Many librarians would not realize the books were by the same person.

Grace was still trying to keep peace in the house, though, and was ready to do whatever it took to keep Flavius happy.

"I'll write my books and use 'Grace

Livingston Hill-Lutz,'" she compromised. "The people who are used to reading my books are used to 'Hill.' This way it will be easier for them to know I am the author."

Apparently Flavius was satisfied with this arrangement, and Grace used the combination name on several of her next books.

—6—

"Where Do You Get Your Ideas?"

*I*t was now 1914 and war in Europe seemed certain. Many Americans still felt, however, that our country could stay out of the fighting, thanks to the wide Atlantic Ocean that separated us from the Continent.

In Swarthmore, Pennsylvania, Grace's girls were growing up. Grace had homeschooled them both until Margaret was 11 and Ruth 8. They had then started going to the public schools. Both were good students, and had also kept up with their music under Flavius. Now Margaret was a senior in high school, ready to graduate.

Grace's office door was always open, even when she was working hard on a new book. She wrote directly on the typewriter, and had thought out her stories and knew her characters so well that she did not have to do much rewriting.

Margaret and Ruth, and often some of their friends, would at times stand behind Grace's typewriter, eagerly grabbing each new sheet as it came from the machine. They would read the latest developments in the new book aloud and give their own comments.

"This reminds me of when I was a little girl," Grace told them. "I used to stand behind Auntie Belle's typewriter and read her stories as she wrote them."

Having several pairs of eyes on her as she worked apparently did not bother Grace's concentration on what she was writing. Even when she was a girl and reading items to her father, she had been able to come back to the story she was working on after the diversion. And with young people around, it was a good ability to have!

She had always liked being with young people, and she encouraged her girls to bring their many friends home. There was now a tennis court in the yard, so they could enjoy the game just as she had when she was growing up.

Young people liked Grace as much as she liked them. They often brought some of their problems to her and asked her advice. It was a little like having a second mother. Besides, they all knew there would always be food at her house for them!

When anyone asked her how she had prepared herself to be a writer, and how she went about writing her books, she was at a loss to explain.

"I don't know," she would admit. "I never

did anything to prepare myself to be a writer. If you have something to say, you just sit down and say it!"

That may have made sense to Grace, but it was not much help to the students and reporters who had asked her the questions!

As the girls grew and were more help to Grace, the Lutzes' marriage was fast going the other way. Flavius left more and more frequently now, and stayed away longer each time. Often he missed the lessons he was supposed to give his students, and sometimes he did not even show up to play the organ at church. Fortunately, Margaret was able to fill in for him.

When Flavius did come home, he was more critical than usual of everyone in the family, causing tension and unhappiness to Grace and the others.

Finally, Flavius left again, and this time both he and Grace knew he would not be back. The two would not live together as man and wife any more.

Grace never talked much about this sad second marriage, even to close friends. Divorce was never considered, and it is not known whether Flavius finally said, "I'm leaving for good," or if Grace lost patience with his actions and told him to leave. It might have been a joint decision that this was the only way to solve their problems.

The marriage had been a mistake from the start—a disaster for both Grace and Flavius, although Grace, at least, had tried to make it work. Flavius, too, had had spurts of being a charming husband and father to the girls.

Even so, this marriage had not come close to being the happy time she remembered from her seven years as Frank Hill's wife. She may have felt a sense of relief and freedom to have Flavius gone for good.

The question of what name to use on her books came up again.

"There is a lot of anti-German feeling right now," her publisher said. "And 'Lutz' is German. The use of two names is awkward, too. Would you consider going back to 'Grace Livingston Hill'?"

Grace was quick to agree. She dropped the "Lutz" from her name and always referred to herself as "Mrs. Hill."

Some libraries and book reviewers kept on listing her books under "Hill-Lutz" since she was still legally "Mrs. Lutz." But even this eventually stopped as Grace refused to use her second husband's name and the books actually used only "Hill."

In the midst of this busy life, Grace was invited to come to a special series of Bible studies. She hesitated. She had been a Christian all her life, had lived with two preachers, and probably knew the Bible as well as anyone. In the end, though, she decided to go.

A new method was used to teach this study. It had begun in Great Britain and spread to the United States. It centered on the Gospel of John and the seven miracles proving Jesus is definitely God's Son.

Suddenly Grace saw the Bible in a new light. This new enthusiasm brought her to a new and deeper relationship with the Lord, and a desire to serve Him more.

"God gave me my gifts," she said. "I will do all I can to show Him how grateful I am to Him." She came home determined and eager to be a better witness for Christ.

"I'm going to spend more of my time and effort spreading Christ's gospel," she told her girls.

How to do this was clear to Grace. She would put the message of salvation in her novels from now on, and would make it so plain that any reader could understand.

By now Grace's name was becoming well known in Christian circles. She was writing two or three books a year and was back with her original publisher, J. B. Lippincott. Her books were listed on "suggested reading" lists of many religious organizations of the time, representing different creeds.

Grace's novels were reaching more readers than any preacher could hope to reach from his pulpit, and some of her readers had never been in a church. They did not know about God's salvation plan, but they would read a novel, it seemed, if it were exciting and interesting enough. And Grace's novels all were!

Until now her novels had had Christian characters but had not stressed the way of salvation. Now she determined that she would include it in every book she wrote from now on.

However, when Grace took her next book, *A Voice in the Wilderness*, to Lippincott, they objected to her new way of putting the salvation message so openly.

"That will have to be toned down!" they told her.

Grace set her jaw and squared her shoulders. "If you won't publish it like it is, I'll take it elsewhere!"

Apparently Lippincott would not change its mind, and Grace would not budge from her position. The book would be printed as she had written it or it would not be printed at all! It was a firm deadlock!

Fortunately, there was no shortage of other publishers who were happy to have a writer like Grace Livingston Hill who could write two or three books a year and have an eager audience always waiting for the next one.

Harper Brothers brought out *A Voice in the Wilderness* just as Grace had written it.

For her novels, Grace often took characters

from real life, disguising them with new names and new settings. Usually she took people she liked and was kind to them as she put them into her fiction. Both Grace's father and mother can be easily seen in her books, and they are always treated gently and positively.

But she was not always nice to her characters! *A Voice in the Wilderness* had an example of how she treated those she did not like in real life.

In the novel, a preacher on vacation is an obnoxious character who does not really believe in Christ's atonement or in hell. He comes to a small Western town to get away from "prayers, Bible reading and sermons." To impress the heroine, he preaches to a congregation with several rough cowboys in it.

The cowboys do not like his message and one by one leave the room. They wait for the preacher outside and end up rudely dunking him in a pond as a way to get him to change his preaching—and his mind.

The real preacher who was the pattern for this character in the book had preached at Grace's church one Sunday before she wrote the novel. His ideas, like those of the fictional preacher, were not what Grace liked or knew about Biblical truths.

She came home from that church service upset and angry.

"But what can I do about it?" she may have

wondered. "I may not be able to do anything about *him*, but I can put him in a book! It will show my readers how I stand and how disappointed I am about this kind of preaching!"

Dunking the real preacher might have been more to Grace's liking than just putting him in a book, but there was always the chance he would read it and recognize himself. Or someone else might read the book, realize he was the preacher in the story, and tell him about it.

It was the best Grace could do, but she left no doubt as to how she felt about such "modern" preaching!

A Voice in the Wilderness was only one of Grace's many books that began with something she knew and had experienced. She was always alert for story ideas, and an incident at home or church, overheard conversations or casual remarks by friends, could start her active imagination working. Sometimes it seemed that even a Bible verse or story could end up being the start of one of Grace's novels.

The girls were now going on with their education at Swarthmore College, just as Grace had hoped they would when she built the stone house there. Both girls were also keeping up with their music, so the big house was always a busy place with young voices laughing, talking, or singing. It was activity that Grace loved.

The girls had taken over the music school

that Flavius had left behind and seemed to have almost as much pep and vitality as their mother had always had.

But the war was coming closer to America, and no one seemed able to stop our country's getting involved in it despite the distance between us and France where the fighting was going on.

7

The Power of Her Books

*A*merica finally did get into World War I in April 1917. It was called "The War to End Wars," and both Margaret and Ruth saw many of their men friends heading off to training camps. One of these was Gordon Munce, who had become a close friend of Ruth's.

That same year Harper Brothers brought out Grace's new book, *The Witness*.

The plot in this book was in part borrowed from the Biblical account of Stephen's stoning, with Saul as a witness—the Saul who eventually became Paul, one of the great early Christian leaders.

In fact, Grace named her dead Christian "Stephen," and the hero, who sees him die while trying to save others in a theater fire, is called "Paul." The book follows the modern Paul's life afterward as he learns more about the Lord whom Stephen served and comes to believe for himself, and eventually becomes a minister.

In the front of this book Grace put the Bible verse: "He who believeth on the Son of God hath the witness in himself. (1 John 5:10)"

Grace dedicated the book to her mother, ". . . whose helpful criticism and loving encouragement have been with me through the years." Now she had dedicated a book to each of her parents, and her mother was very much alive to see and appreciate it.

While most of Grace's books were romances, usually told from a woman's point of view, *The Witness* was definitely a man's book. It was exciting, with romance less important than action and character. Readers found the book not only fun to read but many had their lives changed by it, and they did not hesitate to tell Grace so in letters they wrote her.

The Witness was, perhaps, Grace's most popular book, judging from the number of letters she received from readers who had been touched by it. Thousands of letters came, praising the book and telling her exactly how it had helped. Some had not been Christians before reading *The Witness* but had found the Lord through its story. Others admitted to having drifted away from their Christian faith and having come back to it while reading the book.

Many of those who wrote were men, who ordinarily did not read novels—because novels were thought to be for women and not for real men! But the men had benefited from this one and now were eager Grace Livingston Hill fans!

Most of the letters Grace received were from ordinary people who were neither rich nor well known in the world. But one man, John Wanamaker, was both well known and rich.

The founder of the big department store in Philadelphia, he did more than praise the book and its author—he gave away hundreds of copies to friends, relatives and employees. He also had an attractive display of the book in one of his store windows across from City Hall.

In giving a copy to a friend, Mr. Wanamaker wrote, "I am also sending you a book that I read more than two years ago which gave me a blessing in the sense of the presence of God with us in our daily lives."

The popularity and impact on readers of *The Witness* lasted long after the book first came out. Years later Grace had people bring her their old copies to autograph, revealing the power of that book in their lives.

Naturally she was pleased with the response from people who had been helped by her writing, but she was also awed at the stacks of letters.

"I feel an obligation to answer all these letters," she told her daughters, "and to answer all their questions. But I'm going to need help. I can't do it alone!"

Margaret and Ruth agreed to help, but they

wrote only what Grace told them to. Later Grace would have to hire a secretary, Robert Cressy, who stayed with her for several years before going on to become a minister himself.

The success of *The Witness* was not lost on Lippincott. They quickly asked Grace to come back to them, and agreed that from then on they would not change a word of what she had written.

Grace agreed, and from then on she had only the one publisher—and nothing she put down was changed.

No one was sure what made Grace's books so popular with readers. None of her novels ever made the "Best Seller List" but all sold well, and it was obvious from her mail that they had been read and loved, not bought just for displaying on a bookshelf.

It may have been Grace's simple style, easily read by the young people she aimed the books for as well as by older readers. It may have been partly the fact that she never used bad language, or it may just have been that people wanted the kind of reading matter that Grace gave them. There was no doubt, though, that her readers welcomed the salvation message in fiction, and the writers who tried to copy her never quite equaled her popularity.

As the fighting went on overseas, Grace was often asked her opinion of the war. In one interview, she blamed the war on the sins of the whole world, especially that of ignoring God. She pleaded for the people at home to come as close to God as some of the soldiers had during battle.

Grace's novels now mentioned the war, and were as up-to-date as she could make them. One critic claimed she used the same formula over and over but made each story different by simply basing the themes around current events.

To keep pace with what was happening, Grace's books dealt with the problems of the soldiers at the front dreaming of home, adventures of secret service agents, and the intrigues of spies. The books were exciting and always turned out well for the heroine and hero.

Asked once why she had all her books end so happily, Grace smiled. "I feel there is enough sadness and sorrow in the world, so I try to end my books as beautifully as possible—since that is God's way and the best way."

Having her novels end happily did not mean that Grace led a sheltered life and knew nothing about poverty, gambling, cheating, and other sins that were everywhere in the world. These she put into her books, too, but she never gave them the final victory! That was for Jesus and His people!

After the war ended, Grace was asked by Evangeline Booth, daughter of the founder of the Salvation Army and its current Commander, to write a historical account of the Army's role in the war.

In her preface to *The War Romance of the Salvation Army*, Grace tells readers of how she came to agree to meet with Evangeline. She was both curious and doubtful, not sure whether she was to attempt to write this book or not.

When Evangeline took her hand, though, and looked at her face, Grace wanted to write the book "more than any work that had ever come to my hand. I only wondered if I was worthy." The story grabbed her from the start, and the two women seemed to think as one.

"I am too busy with other duties to write the book myself," Commander Booth told Grace. "But the public wants a book about our role in the war. I need a writer to work with me on it. There is plenty of material and documentation to base the book on. The big job will be to go through it and decide what to include and what can be left out."

The women went to work. The Salvation Army had been active in the war from the start, trying hard to create a home away from home for the boys "over there." They had done this from trucks, in hut-like buildings, and wherever they could get to in France. Many of the American soldiers had never been away from home before, let alone in a foreign country where they could not understand the language. The Salvation Army "lassies" did their best to bring back memories of home.

The enemy knew the value of the Salvation Army to the morale of American troops. Grace opens the book with a dramatic account of the burning of the Salvation Army Training School in New York City. This was followed by an attempt to kill Commander Booth.

An enemy spy once tried to be friendly to Evangeline, and after a while casually asked, "Where are the Salvation Army workers now in France?" He knew that if the Salvation Army Workers were there, American troops would be too.

Fortunately, Evangeline was smart enough not to give any information but to say, "Wherever they are most needed." The man was arrested that same night along with five other spies.

Grace worked hard on the book; it ended up being one of her longest. However, it was only her second nonfiction book, and trying to make the reader see places that she herself had never been was a real problem.

Fortunately, Evangeline had many photographs and other illustrations to show Grace what the equipment, buildings and workers looked like as they tried to make a homelike place for the troops to come to relax. The "lassies" sewed on buttons, gave the men homemade donuts and coffee, and listened to them talk of home and their families.

There was also a more solemn side of the Salvation Army's work in the field.

It came before the soldiers were to move up to the front or go "over the top." ("Over the top" was the expression to describe the men climbing out of the deep trenches where they had been living and trying to cross the barbwired "no man's land" to rout the enemy out of their trenches.)

Before the orders came to move out, the Salvation Army moved among the men. They offered prayers and religious services, helped write letters home that might be that soldier's last words to his loved ones, and encouraged the men in their Christian faith.

The War Romance of the Salvation Army was a tribute to the organization and its Christian work, and to the people who were part of it.

The book came out in 1919 "by Evangeline Booth and Grace Livingston Hill."

Grace did not give all her time that year to the Salvation Army story. In 1918 she wrote *The Enchanted Barn* which was her best-selling book, although she always thought of *The Witness* as her best.

The war ended in victory for the Allies, but it was also the end of an era. A new time was beginning in America and around the world.

8

New Forms of Outreach

*T*he end of the war in Europe meant the end of an era and way of life in America. Before the war, the country had been mostly rural. But boys who had never been more than a few miles from home went to training camps far away, and eventually to a country with one of the world's busiest and most famous cities: Paris.

In fact, one of the popular songs that came out after the war showed the change. "How Are Ya Goin' to Keep 'Em Down on the Farm After They've Seen Paree?" summed up the fears of a lot of parents of recently discharged soldiers.

The men came home having met people with lives different from their own quiet ones, and the farm life was not enough for many of them.

When war came, men who had not joined the army had moved with their families to the cities to work in factories that made the guns, tanks and ships for the war. They had learned new ways, too, and made new friends.

When World War I started, America was a

country where the church was a very important part of life for many people. It was not only a place to worship but also the center of their social life.

Now, with the war over, other kinds of entertainment were coming. The automobile could take people away from their small towns into cities with glittering amusements. It was the beginning of what would be called "The Roaring Twenties" or "The Jazz Age."

Life was changing for Grace, too. Her daughters were now young women; her mother and Auntie Belle were growing old.

Ruth was the first to marry. She and Gordon Munce lived with Grace for a time, then found a home of their own. Later, when Ruth got sick and needed care, they moved back in with Grace. Grace's family was still close by, the way she wanted it.

With all the changes around her, Grace changed the plots of her novels to keep up with the times and the newspaper headlines. But even in the midst of these times, she kept writing about moral, Christian characters, about high ideals and gracious living. None of her books had any of the dirty language that was often appearing in other novels, and no Grace Livingston Hill book had anything but romantic love.

"Grace," some people said, "you'll have to change your style of writing. If you don't, it could mean the end of your career! People don't want to hear what you're saying—not today!"

But Grace had no intention of changing. And she was right! Her books were more popular than ever. Despite the world's rush and frenzy to find new thrills and excitement, Grace began getting more and more letters from people who wanted to read about Christian characters and they thanked her for giving them this kind of reading.

Many of these letters of thanks came from veterans of the fighting. One man declared that meeting a character of Grace's stories was like "touching a friendly hand in the groping black of a 'no man's land' sortie on a cold, black night."

Not only were Grace's stories still popular in book form, many were also being printed in family magazines as serials. The editors saw that they made good reading for all ages.

Grace's books dealt with current events. One book was about graft and racketeering; another showed the false "fun" of the whirlwind social life of the rich, as the heroine tried it and found it empty.

It was near the middle of that tumultuous decade that a new ministry opened up for Grace. It was one she would always think of as one of her main purposes in life.

While she was having a new addition put on the stone house, Grace met the workers.

They were Italian immigrants who lived in a small community just outside Swarthmore. The men were skilled stone masons and worked at a quarry near their homes.

As the men worked, they apparently heard Margaret and Ruth playing their music, and one came to the door to ask Grace for a special favor.

"Would you and your daughters come and give a concert for our people?" he asked.

If the suggestion surprised Grace, she did not show it. She and the girls agreed to give a concert the following Sunday in a field near the Italian community. To Grace's delight, more than 200 enthusiastic people were there waiting for them, including many children.

The girls knew their audience, and the music they played was by Italian composers that the immigrants would easily recognize.

As she looked around at the audience, Grace was suddenly aware of another need here. There was no church for the people!

When the concert was over, Grace spoke to the parents. "Would you allow me to come and have a Sunday school for your children?" she asked.

The parents were eager, and the first class was set to start in three weeks.

Grace sent her own car and driver (she never learned to drive herself) each week to pick up the children. Many were dirty, but she was able to look past their grimy faces and see that they were children who needed to hear about Jesus.

The Italian immigrants welcomed Grace into their homes and sometimes invited her to their parties. Despite the differences in customs and language, she and they got along well. The people were anxious to share their culture with her and tried to do things they thought would please her.

For herself, Grace learned firsthand about a way of life she had not known before. She saw close-up the problems the people had as they tried to adjust to American life.

At first Grace just rented a room near the Italian community for the Sunday school, but it began to grow. People from outside the community were also coming, and it was time to find a larger, permanent place to meet. Someone suggested the Old Leiper Church.

The small church building, near Leiperville and named for the well-known Philadelphia family who had helped with its early years, was an old stone structure. It was set among trees near its old cemetery.

The building dated back to 1848, but as the people in the area moved to the city, the membership dropped. When the church could not get a regular minister, the people who were left decided to join a city church.

The building had been empty for years and

was in need of repairs. Actually, though, it was in pretty good shape, thanks to its being made of stone with a slate roof. Even some of the stained glass windows were still intact.

Inside, the church was plain, almost bare, with no carpet on the floor and with hard pews. But it looked perfect to Grace and she quickly got permission to use it for her Sunday school class.

One of the men who helped repair the church, and to keep it up even after Grace died, was Santino Di Mateo, called "Sunday" by his friends because he was always in church on Sundays.

When the Old Leiper Church opened its doors again in 1926, it was considered a "mission church" by the Presbytery. Grace taught Sunday school classes and Bible study for adults on Monday nights. She found a local minister, Rev. William Allan Dean, who could come and lead weekly Bible lessons. She also brought in outside speakers and ministers for church services.

Grace did other things for the church, too. She donated books for the "Library Corner." Many of them were her own, of course, but there were also books by other authors that she felt were good reading for Christians.

She also wrote Sunday school lessons and pageants for the children and young people of the church to give. She acted as director for these as well.

One play, a Christmas one titled "The Best Birthday," was so popular with all the people of the church that it was given every Christmas for years. Finally Grace had it published so other Sunday schools could put it on also.

Grace's big Lincoln car, now driven by Sunday, and later by his son, became a sort of "taxi," as one woman put it. The car took people to church, to the doctor's, or to the hospital if necessary, and was always ready to be used in the Lord's work. And the garden Grace had planted now furnished flowers for the church and to take to the sick.

But the greatest contribution Grace made to the Old Leiper Church was to pay all its bills, including expenses for visiting speakers. She did this from the money she got while on her speaking tours.

Like her Auntie Belle, Grace was now popular as a speaker at churches and other religious groups.

In the big car, which she called "my only luxury," Grace traveled several hundred miles a week. She visited churches in Pittsburgh, Harrisburg, and Washington, D.C. She also went to Canada and various cities in the Midwest. She felt an obligation to be a moral leader for young people and was as popular with them in person as she was through her many books.

Because she spoke to so many groups over such a wide area, she could not always write a new talk for each speech, but if people realized it, they did not say so.

She did refuse to call her talks "lectures," though. "I do not lecture," she said emphatically.

Instead, knowing that some of her listeners had read all her books, she summarized each of them into a few pages so she could give a review of several.

With her natural flair for the dramatic, Grace could make the characters come to life in front of her audience. She talked informally to the groups, answering all their questions before leaving to go home or on to the next church.

When Grace was asked what her fee for speaking would be, she always said, "There is no fee."

When those who had invited her protested, she would add, "You can pay my expenses. And if you want, you may make a contribution to the Old Leiper Church and its work. I do not need the money for myself. My writing earns me a very nice living, adequate for my needs."

The gifts given Grace were enough to handle the expenses of the old stone church she loved so much.

At the Old Leiper Church, and at her own

church, Grace was always easily identified by the hats she wore. While every woman wore a hat to church, Grace's were big hats. She loved them and had one for each of her outfits. The photo taken for the cover of her books showed her in one of her favorites. Many children remembered her years after she died because of her "trademark" hats that could be seen across the church!

Not everything was happy for Grace during those years, though. Within the span of a few weeks both her uncle and her cousin, one whom she had gotten quite close to despite his being younger, died. Her own mother also died.

It was a hard time for Grace, but to add to her sorrow Auntie Belle left to go to California to live with her daughter-in-law.

There had always been a special closeness between Grace and her aunt. Now they had mostly letters to rely on. Auntie Belle finished her novel *An Interrupted Night* and asked Grace to write the foreword for it. She also mentioned to Grace that she was thinking of a "book of memories."

"But you will have to do most of the work if it is ever to see print," Auntie Belle said. "I'm just so tired."

Belle, now in her eighties, was in pain from a broken hip that did not seem to heal. She was often in bed, and was also discouraged about the trend of society that she saw happening around her. It was easy for her to slip into remembering the better days when she was younger and healthy and the world seemed more serene and comfortable.

"There is no place for my books in the world today," she told Grace when Grace wanted her to start another Christian novel. "The things I have to say are no longer popular. Even Christ is not popular in the world today."

The book, *Memories of Yesterday*, which Grace edited for Auntie Belle, came out in 1931. But Belle had been right when she predicted she would not see it in print. She died in 1930.

And now a new era was starting for Grace and America. It began with the stock market crash in 1929 that wiped out many fortunes. The time would be called "The Great Depression."

—9—

The Busy 1930s

To help ease the sadness of losing so many close relatives, Grace threw herself into her writing. She had always worked long hours, but now she worked even harder. The 1930s were her busiest time. In ten years she published 30 books, all over 300 pages long. It was a feat most writers could only dream of.

Grace's family was changing, too. Although she had lost relatives, she was also gaining new ones. Margaret was married now to Wendell Walker, and for a while both daughters and their husbands lived with her in the big stone house.

When the time came that Margaret wanted her own home, Grace was both hurt and angry.

"There is plenty of room here!" she argued. "You'll be breaking up the family!"

Margaret and Wendell stood firm, but in the end they moved only a short distance from the stone house, so Grace's family was still close by.

Near the beginning of the 1930s, Margaret

and Wendell felt God's call to go as missionaries to rural Kentucky. Grace was upset at the thought of her older daughter, who had been such a close friend, being so far away.

"We feel it is God's will for us," Margaret explained.

Grace could not argue with that! She had been trying to do God's will through her writing and speaking for years. She sent the Walkers off with her blessings and her prayers.

Then the Munces were transferred out of the state by Gordon's employer and had to leave Grace, too. To keep Grace from being alone, her oldest grandson moved in with her. When Ruth and Gordon came back to Swarthmore after only two years, they lived with Grace again and stayed until her death.

Grace's writing was not the only thing that kept her busy. She was still active in the Old Leiper Church. In those days of the Great Depression, many of the people who came to the church had financial problems. Without any fanfare, Grace helped some of them with gifts. She also kept on paying the bills at the church, and kept up her friendship with "Sunday" Di Mateo.

Besides the Old Leiper Church, Grace continued to be active in her own church, in Swarthmore, and sometimes attended services at still another church in the area.

At home, Grace liked to read. She subscribed to more than ten magazines and is said to have read every issue from cover to cover. This reading kept her up to date on what was happening in the world, as well as the problems being faced by the young people she was writing for.

She also liked some of the current fiction writers that she felt were worthy of a Christian's time, but she would not read some of the more "modern" ones where the language and actions were not Christian.

While she still felt movies were evil, she listened to news and good music on the radio when she had the time. And in her cluttered office she spent many hours at her typewriter, of course.

During the 1930s Grace wrote three of her most popular books. *Matched Pearls* came out in 1933; *Beauty for Ashes* in 1935; and *April Gold* in 1939.

Critics, as well as some of her family, always felt *Matched Pearls* was the best work she had done, although Grace always preferred *The Witness*, written years before.

Thousands more letters poured in about her books. They came from men and women, boys and girls, educated people and those with only a few years in school. People from all sorts of backgrounds and professions, not just ministers and church workers, appreciated her books.

Although most letters from readers were

complimentary and thanked Grace for the story that had helped them, the secular critics did not always say nice things about her work. In fact, some of them were very negative, and sometimes they made fun of her "religious" emphasis.

One reviewer for the New York *Times* panned *Beauty for Ashes* this way: "This story is a simple romance, weaving religious sentiment into its everyday talk. Its . . . obvious moral is that happiness lies in the path of righteousness."

About *April Gold* the same newspaper said, "The saccharine flavor . . . is relieved by friendly descriptions. . . . The priggish characters have a chance to show gallantry. For readers who enjoy an all-pervading religious atmosphere, Mrs. Hill's books always fill the bill."

About some of Grace's other books, reviewers wrote, "It is a good story for a Sunday night—if one has been to church." And " . . . a fictional equivalent of a prayer meeting."

This tearing down of her work by critics was not new to Grace. More than fifteen years before, a critic had called one of her books "unbridled sentimentalism" and said the plot was "not even plausible."

Many of the reviewers, however, now added a grudging bit of praise for Grace's work. Even the reviewer of *Beauty for Ashes* ended with a comment that must have pleased her.

The last sentence was an opinion that "this book could safely be put into the hands of any young girl!" Since this was exactly what Grace wanted to happen to her books, even that reviewer was admitting the value of her writings!

Grace kept answering each letter that came to her, now with the help of a secretary as well as her own family. Many of these letters came from young people who asked Grace's advice about their problems, and she gave it to each one, thoughtfully and prayerfully.

In 1936 the town of Swarthmore made up a *Souvenir Directory*, listing everyone living in the town as well as its businesses. Better-known citizens were given more than just a mention. Naturally Grace was one of those spotlighted since she was well known outside the town.

The *Directory* contained a page with the heading "Noted Author a Resident of Swarthmore." The page included a picture of the old stone house where Grace had lived so much of her life, surrounded by big trees. There was also a picture of two of her grandchildren, but there was no picture of her.

Not allowing her picture to be included was typical of Grace's lack of pretense about herself and her love of showing off her family instead. She still lived quietly without attracting attention to herself. It is likely that many people in the town had never connected the well-known writer of Christian fiction with this quiet woman who worked so hard for the Lord in the churches.

Included in this *Directory* were parts of two letters from young men, both college students, written to Grace. One said, "Your stories leave one feeling uplifted without being bored. . . . They are so true to those vital things of our holy faith."

The other young man had written, "Before I read your books, religion had no interest for me, but since I read them, my eyes have been opened."

These were the kind of letters that were Grace's true "payment" for her work. These letters proved that her books were helping readers to know the Lord—and *that* had always been her main objective!

Readers like these kept Grace writing, sometimes until 2 or 3 a.m., and going out to speak to groups about her writing and to give her witness for the Lord.

During this time Grace also wrote several novels using her mother's maiden name, Marcia Macdonald, as her pen name. It was another tribute to her mother and her help through the years.

She even tried writing some short stories again. These were brought out by Lippincott, each in its own paperback edition. They did not get much publicity and were never as popular with readers as Grace's novels were.

Since these stories had each been printed like a thin book, the total number of "books" Grace wrote during her life was never agreed upon by reporters. The number given ranges from 71 to more than 100! It depends on whether the reporter counted the short stories as separate works or not, as well as when he started his count of Grace's books. Some included her very early ones while others began their roster later.

In 1976 some of Grace's short stories were gathered together into a hardcover volume. The editor explained to readers that these had not been reprinted till then because only one or two copies of each one had been located.

At her death, one magazine called Grace "indefatigable," and no matter how the critics counted her books, it was obvious she had not wasted any of the time God had given her on earth.

In 1939, when another book, *Patricia*, came out, Grace was interviewed for a long article by a *Time* magazine reporter. She was now 74 years old, but the reporter admiringly said she could easily pass for 60. She had "a quick step, full firm voice, deep laugh, and only slightly grayed hair."

"What are your thoughts about the future of the world?" the reporter asked as the interview went on.

Grace did not hesitate to tell him, even though she knew her opinion was not a popular one.

"I think the coming of the anti-Christ is very near. I think three or four possibilities are alive right now!"

The reporter did not write the names of those people Grace felt were so evil, but with Hitler, Mussolini and Stalin now feared dictators, it is likely that Grace had all of them in mind as World War II loomed.

— 10 —

A Fruitful Writer to the End

*T*he coming of World War II was a blow to Grace. She had lived through one awful war, and now another, even bigger and crueler, was going on. She loved peace and wanted it for the whole world.

The stories in the newspapers and on the radio of the horrors and heartless atrocities being done in Europe and the Far East—sometimes by men who professed to being Christian—upset her. The world was changing so fast, and not in the direction Grace would like. This world was no longer the happy, secure place she had known for most of her life.

Grace was getting older, too. When Pearl Harbor was bombed by the Japanese on December 7, 1941, she was 75 years old. Some of the great energy she had always had seemed to be leaving her.

People who knew Grace only through her books would not have noticed any slowing down, though. In 1940, 1941, 1942 and 1943 Grace published three books a year.

In 1944 and 1945, though, she produced only two books each year, and in 1946 she was able to write only one novel.

New styles of writing were becoming popular and were on topics never talked about when Grace was growing up. "Realistic" and "modern" they were called. Grace knew they were not what a Christian should read, and she kept to her old ways and style.

In a foreword to *The Spice Box* in 1943, the editor reminded readers that "gentle wisdom and gracious living have always been connected with the books by Grace Livingston Hill."

Grace was determined they would stay that way, no matter what other writers of the day did or how popular their books became. Not making the "Best Seller" list did not bother her. She only wanted to help readers find a Savior or to strengthen their faith.

Jean Karr, a woman who wrote about Grace in the New York *Times*, said about her books that they were "more than a pleasant pastime for thousands of people, they were object lessons in clean living and thinking."

Staying to her own style of Christian writing did not mean that Grace's books were not still up-to-date. She kept on changing her plots, characters and settings to keep up with the times.

Now Grace's books mentioned the war, and several dealt directly with it and the problems it brought. There was nothing old-fashioned about Grace's books!

One, *A Girl to Come Home To*, was about a veteran who had seen the bloody fighting first-hand and been disillusioned, just as Grace herself had been. The book told the story of his finding his faith again when he came home. Perhaps she found it personally helpful to write an encouraging book right then.

A Girl to Come Home To brought in more letters, many from veterans who recognized the same situation in their own lives. They wrote to thank Grace for writing about the problems so that people who had never experienced life under fire, or been bombed, could understand something of what they were struggling with as they came back to their hometowns and old friends and family.

The years of constant work were taking more and more of a toll on Grace's health and energy, though. From the time Frank had died and left her with two small girls to support and raise until now, she had been busy long hours every day with her family, her church, and her calling to write.

"In fifty years I have not had a real vacation," Grace told one interviewer.

One of the things Grace had enjoyed in her career was the speaking times when she shared her faith and work with other Christians. It was one of the last things she wanted to give up, but in 1945, when she was 79 years old, she was too worn out to keep on. She did not feel up to traveling so much and, reluctantly, she had to start turning down the invitations to speak that were coming to her.

Then, on August 6 and again on August 9, 1945, Grace and America had another shock. The United States dropped two atomic bombs on Japan. This new, unbelievably powerful weapon was not a complete surprise to the military, but to Grace it seemed like the last straw. She could not think of that being done by a Christian nation, even though it brought on a quick end to the war and may have saved many lives.

"I don't belong down here any more," she told a friend.

Grace's health got worse. By fall of 1946 it was obviously failing fast. Doctors found that she had cancer, a dreaded disease with few treatments. They operated to remove the cancer but the operation took more of Grace's dwindling strength.

In those days, cancer was not talked about openly, only in fearful whispers, so most of Grace's readers and friends did not know what her real problem was or how serious it was.

More and more now, Grace's mind drifted to the past, as her Auntie Belle's had done. She had been much happier then, and she yearned to be back when those she loved were still alive and she was at the height of her energy and drive.

The big stone house was still an active place, with grandchildren running around. But Grace was no longer the one in charge. Ruth and her husband were the ones who took care of the house—and of Grace.

Strangely, though, when Grace sat down at her typewriter to work on her latest novel, her mind seemed to clear, and she was as completely immersed in her writing's plot and characters as she had ever been. It was as though she had never been away from her desk.

But the time she could spend at the typewriter got shorter and shorter each week. Sometimes she had to have Ruth help her back to bed after writing only a few pages. Her bedroom and her study were next to each other, and she also had a couch she could rest on. Her fabulous energy was running out fast now.

Yet when her publisher asked her to sign a new contract for two books a year, Grace signed. She believed she would be able to honor it.

In January 1947, Grace's last book came out. *Where Two Ways Meet* was her final complete book, although she was already at work on another.

Early in February, Grace gave her last interview, in her home.

The interviewer asked many questions

about Grace's career as a Christian writer, and in the article called her "one of America's best loved novelists, as well as the most prolific." He estimated that more than four million of Grace's novels had been printed in America alone. His estimate did not include later reprints and those published in other countries, which may have almost doubled the number of Grace Livingston Hill books in the world.

When the interviewer asked Grace how she had been able to hold readers through several generations, she told him, "Because I am not writing just for the sake of writing. I have attempted to convey . . . a message which God has given, and to convey that message with whatever abilities were given to me. Whatever I've been able to accomplish has been God's doing. I've tried to follow His teaching in all my writing and thoughts."

Grace did not live long enough to see that interview published. On February 23, 1947, she went from this world where she no longer felt at home to the next where she knew her Savior was waiting. She left behind a half-finished book, *Mary Arden*, which Ruth finished, using Grace's style.

"Where shall we hold Mother's funeral?" her family wondered.

It would have been logical to have the last services at the Old Leiper Church that Grace had loved and supported for so long, but that was a very small building and it was obvious that there would be hundreds of people coming for the funeral.

Because "cancer" was never mentioned in obituaries then, the cause of Grace's death was given as "a general breakdown due to her advanced years and to her having worked hard."

Thousands of letters and cards came from stunned readers who felt they knew Grace personally even though they had never met her. Many of these people had read all of Grace's books and had been looking forward to many more. They could not believe their favorite writer was gone.

It was quite clear that even Grace's church in Swarthmore would not be large enough for all the people who wanted to pay their last respects to the woman who had given them so many hours of pleasure and had strengthened their faith. The decision, therefore, was to hold Grace's last rites at the large and well-known Tenth Presbyterian Church in Philadelphia.

The funeral was both sad and triumphant. Grace's friends and readers were sorry to no longer have her books to look forward to, but they also knew she was with the Lord she had lovingly served.

The Rev. Allan Dean, the pastor who had come for years to the Old Leiper Church to teach Monday night Bible classes, conducted the funeral. He was helped by Grace's old secretary, Robert Cressy, now a minister, too.

The hundreds of people who crowded into the church heard Mr. Dean end the service by reading from Revelation 5:11–12. "I heard the voice of many angels saying with a loud voice, Worthy is the Lamb that was slain to receive power, and riches, and wisdom, and strength, and honor, and glory, and blessing."

He then told the congregation, "Let us rejoice for her who joins that song today."

It was a fitting final tribute to Grace's life on earth.

Epilogue

Grace Livingston Hill is dead, her typewriter covered. Yet today, more than a half century later, her books are still very much alive.

In many libraries you still find them on the shelves—back away from the more modern novels, but still there. Some are in their original covers, now worn, stained and sometimes mended. The pages are often dog-eared and faded. But readers keep checking them out.

Many Grace Livingston Hill books are still available in colorful paperback reprints. They are on the racks in bookstores and drugstores. It has been estimated that Grace has had as many or more books reprinted as any other author of her day.

If you read a Grace Livingston Hill book (and we hope you will), the language will sound formal and stilted. There is no slang. The characters may sometimes seem "too good to be true." If you read on, though, you will find they were not "saints." They were not living in ivory towers or some private biosphere; they were living in the world the way it was in their day, with all its evils and temptations.

The novels will give you an insight into what life was like then. They will tell you how the people worked, dressed and amused themselves. They will tell you the problems Christians like you faced. They too struggled to do right and to live the way the Lord wanted them to.

Many of their problems will seem unimportant to you who live in a world where AIDS, homosexuality and racism abound. But the problems Grace's characters faced were as real and vital to them as these are to you. The answer then was the same as it is today: making Jesus Christ Lord of your life in all areas.

And that is what Grace Livingston Hill and her work were all about.